The Art of the Recruiter Message

How to Master the Craft of Recruiter Outreach over InMail, Email, Text Message

Jonathan Kidder

Table of Contents

Introduction

As with some other professions, recruiters are self-developed and taught how to recruit once they've started on the job.

Most recruiters have to learn how to message leads on their own and are sometimes taught the wrong things.

For example, many agency-based recruiters are tracked on daily metrics – i.e. how many candidates did you reach out to today? [Period]

Recruiters get praised on getting high metrics but in turn they may be learning how to over spam the market. Spamming unfortunately is a common occurrence in our field.

Many recruiters are taught to mass message. You can have the best tool and resources available but you may miss out on exceptional talent by sticking with "vanilla based" recruiter templates.

With the recruiting market being more competitive than ever, you must master the basics of crafting tailored recruiter messages. Focusing more on quality over quantity will help differentiate yourself from a sea of other recruiters online.

The frustration that recruiters face is feeling as if they put in the necessary hours to source and approach qualified candidates, but they don't receive a high response rate. You can put in a ton of hours as a recruiter but that won't necessarily translate to getting a hire.

It takes an ART when reaching out to candidates online, whether it's over InMail, email, or text message. You will need to craft an appropriate message that will produce a response from a passive candidate.

In the following pages, you'll discover techniques for engaging qualified candidates, building recruiter-candidate relationships and repeatedly matching the perfect candidate to the perfect position. Due to high demand, most candidates in niche fields can afford to be passive. So, you will need to capture their attention with a call to action and create an emotionally engaging message.

Continue reading to learn how to engage your targeted audience and communicate in such a compelling way that clients rely on you as a top producing recruiter.

In the Art of the Recruiter Message, you'll learn how to:

- Understand best practices in outreach methods.
- Grabbing a potential leads attention.
- Improving chances of engagement.
- Learning how to follow up with leads.
- Drafting, creating, and implementing 25+ reusable recruiter templates.
- Personalizing recruiter templates.
- Tracking, deliverability, and AI automation tools in the market.
- How to create email drip campaigns and mail merges effectively.

Chapter 1: Know Your Targets

Isn't it interesting how successful and rewarding relationships of any kind ultimately boil down to having exceptional communication skills?

Whether you're developing a relationship with a new client, building rapport with candidates, or even reaching out to strangers to grab the attention of that prime target audience—you must first understand what exactly makes a specific audience tick, regardless if communication transpires through speaking or writing.

Let's face it, recruiters wear many hats and time is of the essence. So, knowing and understanding your target audience and getting their attention long enough to develop a relationship can separate the average recruiter from the exceptional one.

Practically all recruiters have experienced staring at lingering unfilled job positions and low response rates to outreach attempts.

Undoubtedly, ample time and effort were contributed but nonetheless, deadlines/goals were missed, budgets depleted, all without a positive outcome.

While the cause may have been attributed to a lackluster job announcement, or a shortage of qualified candidates, the following tips can help you experience outstanding candidate response and hiring rates in the future.

Knowing Your Target Audience is Key
Undoubtedly, a strong recruiter must have excellent marketing skills to reach their target audience.

Conducting research and talent map that will enable you to reach out to that audience is essential to not only attracting the right people, but also enticing them to learn more about what you have to offer.

By familiarizing yourself with their language, tone, habits, and concerns will also provide insight on their preferred modes of communication (email, InMail, direct message, etc.) and how to reach them online (i.e. social media, websites, and job board platforms).

Follow the AIDA Model

The AIDA model was first introduced in 1898 by Elias St. Elmo Lewis. The model was created for marketers as a four-step outreach process to successful convert leads to conversions. This marketing formula can be applied to your recruiting messages to improve response rates. Here's how to break down the formula model.

1. Attention:

The first step is to get the reader's attention. This can be done by way of a relevant subject and email opening line.

2. Interest:

Once you've got your reader's attention, the next step is to pique their interest. This can be done by offering data or social proof that supports your opening statement

3. Desire:

Next, spark desire by telling your reader about the benefits that you can offer them and why they are important to them/ their business.

4. Action:

Finally, once the desire to work with you is aroused, this must be transferred into a clear call to action. Let your reader know what the next steps are and prompt for a response.

Every recruiter template should try and follow this methodology to some degree.

Learn How to Attract Your Ideal Candidate

From the moment you advertise a position, to interviewing and hiring a candidate, the following tips will help you improve your marketing strategy and customize a checklist that produces fast results each time.

Get to Know Your Ideal Candidate

Understanding certain aspects of a target audience will enable you to effectively grab their attention. Besides being familiar with common interests, hobbies, and goals, you need to dive a bit deeper.

For instance, depending on the profession or skill set, what are some specifics they're seeking in a job or company?

It may be scheduling flexibility or having a laid- back work environment. Maybe they are driven by a wide-array of responsibilities, a challenging workload, or opportunities for advancement within a leading-edge company?

Target a candidate persona: who is the ideal applicant?

Identifying a candidate persona helps you understand their ideas and motivators. By creating a detailed profile of your ideal candidate, you can gain insights into what drives them, what their goals and aspirations are, and what values they hold. This information can be invaluable in crafting targeted messaging and recruiting strategies that resonate with your ideal candidates. Ultimately, understanding your candidate persona can help you attract the right talent for your organization and build a strong employer brand (EVP).

Maintain Messaging Consistency

Much like building a brand and maintaining consistency with a logo, creating messaging and job advertising uniformity across all platforms is a must.

While the job advertisement is typically the first impression of your client, you want that "image" to be positive initially as well as throughout subsequent communication.

Identify Your Unique Selling Points

With more competition than ever before, you want to attract those top-talent candidates before someone else does. Make it a point to tailor those job ads and messages in a way that exhibits some personality and encourages a candidate's response.

Selling points may include:
- The position and team itself.
- The company's growth potential
- The company's work culture
- Candidates' opportunity to grow

You can include the average salary comp range that you are targeting as well as the including the job description link in the email.

Of course, salary is a factor with any job, but motivated candidates consider other perks just as important. Be sure to share information about the company, work environment, benefits, and any other unique selling points.

Provide Clear Instructions
While this may seem like a no-brainer, don't forget to provide clear instructions and contact information for interested candidates to respond to you. Creating

brief, interesting, easy- to-read messages will help encourage more qualified candidates to reply.

Junior recruiters may not know all of the requirements or the company's full cycle recruiting. Try and maintain stability and be as truthful with the process as possible.

Why Building a Candidate Relationship is Crucial?
In addition to capturing the attention of your target audience, it's also important to build a relationship with top candidates. This process helps you avoid incorrectly matching candidates to opportunities, which inevitably results in disappointed clients and employee attrition.

A primary factor in building an optimal candidate relationship involves targeting individuals who possess the necessary skill sets, experience and education.

Additionally, the best candidates will be highly motivated and share values that align with a company culture.

Here is a list of the most relevant qualities to build a successful recruiter-candidate relationship.

Transparency

With the goal being to find a candidate who is both qualified and a good-fit personality wise, transparency from both parties is imperative.

As a recruiter, it's your job to provide relevant information about the company, work environment, job responsibilities, and employee benefits.

Further, whether the interview is successful or not, following up with the candidate and providing feedback is much better than ghosting those who didn't make the cut.

Likewise, the candidate must be forthcoming about prior job experience and skills that qualify them for the position as well as their expectations and goals if hired.

Honesty and Openness

As the recruiter-candidate relationship is nurtured, it's important to remain focused when assessing multiple candidates. There will likely be times that you find a candidate very likable personality-wise, but (depending on the role for which you're hiring) a lack of specific skills may disqualify them.

Always be observant and open communicate your concerns with the individual. From the candidate's standpoint, it's also important that they're able to receive constructive criticism, recognizing that it will be helpful down the road.

Advocacy
One of the best ways to strengthen your relationship with candidates is to successfully play the role of advocate. Keep communication lines open and let them know you're rooting for them.

Emphasize the Relationship
Without a doubt, you juggle lots of duties and several candidates on any given day, which may result in the need to pass off candidates to team members. When this occurs, it's crucial that each candidate is assigned to a single recruiter throughout the entire communication process. In addition to preventing candidates from feeling unimportant, it allows a recruiter-candidate relationship to develop so the candidate feels valued.

By practicing these relationship building techniques, it will help you identify candidates who are skilled and enthusiastic, which will ensure a good match.

The more positive a relationship is formed with a candidate, the more likely it will be to find needed talent for future positions and perhaps acquire more referrals as a result.

Why You Must Understand the Role
To attract top candidates, you must understand the position for which you're hiring. Having the knowledge required to accurately convey all important aspects will produce a compelling job description.

Have a conversation with the hiring manager or HR team will help gain a clear understanding of the role and responsibilities involved. By learning details such as why the position is vacant, how it has evolved since the initial implementation, it's correlation with similar roles, and skills required will provide information necessary for the ad creation.

Questions to ask the Hiring Manager:
- Why is this role open?
- What's interesting about this team?
- What makes your culture or environment unique?
- What are the main selling points?
- Ask the team - why do they work here?

Understand Team and Motivators:
- Can you tell me about your team and how it was structured?
- How would you describe your communication style and how do you prefer to receive feedback?
- Are there any particular work styles or personalities you work best with?
- What do you think are the strengths of the current team, and what areas do you think could be improved?
- What are some of your goals for the next few months, and how do you think the team can help you achieve them?
- Are there any team-building activities or events you would like to see happen in the future?

Understand the Environment

It's also a good idea to learn about the overall company environment and persona. While an individual's qualifications may be extraordinary on paper, an aspect that is just as important is finding a good culture fit as well.

Bottom line, an informative job description serves as that initial communication tool with prospective applicants. By clearly explaining the essential duties, skills, and credentials, along with providing company characteristics will help you attract the most desirable candidates.

Gathering Important Candidate Details
Once you properly understand the role, you'll need to identify necessary talents and skills that a qualified candidate should possess.

However, beyond skills, you want to attract motivated candidates, which is achieved through your message, tone and delivery.

What to Look for in a Lead
First and foremost, a candidate should have the skills and experience necessary to perform the required job duties, but other qualifiers include career continuity, interests, a growth mindset, and strong communication skills.

Having the ability to measure these characteristics in a candidate will allow you to improve your outreach and interviewing process and more aptly eliminate non-qualifying candidates.

A quick glance at a candidate's resume and cover letter can reveal a lot about the person. For instance, when an applicant is truly interested in a position, they will likely put in the extra effort to customize the documents to align with a specific role, being sure relevant skills and experience are highlighted quickly.

As a recruiter, you're likely aware of the need to read between the lines and hone in on certain elements.

Below is a list of "across the board" critical details to look for in a candidate.

Relevant Skills

Skill set and experience are apparent, but driven candidates will make a point of emphasizing those most relevant for the role.

Work History

An applicant's work history should encompass the experience required in a job, but just as important is the display of longevity, or career continuity. A resume filled with frequent changes in duties and/or employers is typically a red flag indicating a lack of determination and dedication.

Exceptional Communication

When a qualifying candidate can effectively communicate, they'll be able to effortlessly describe their professional strengths and skills and explain past accomplishments and career experiences, all with a brief objective statement. This level of communication efficiency is a real asset to any company.

Flexibility
In an ever-changing world, flexibility is key. Focus on candidates who not only possess the proper skills but also display a desire and willingness to continually learn and grow.

Authenticity
Skills and previous work experience can look great on a LinkedIn profile or resume, but the best candidate for the job will be confident and authentic during conversations. Be wary of candidates who do not come across as truly genuine or fully committed.

Having the Right Tools
Whether you're new to recruiting or a top producer, you know the importance of having and using digital hiring tools. From software applications that help you organize and prioritize to AI and Boolean

strings that compile search data based on everything from profiles and skill sets to specific online platforms, equipping yourself with the right tools only enhances results for targeting the best prospects.

I recommend checking out these campaign sequencing tools: HireEz, SeekOut, Hireflow, SourceWhale, or WebbTree if you are looking for a complete option. Also, check out TextExpander to automate email templates.

I wrote the book: <u>Top Talent Sourcing for Recruiters</u> that covers all these email automation tools. In this book, I will cover how to mail merge which is a free option.

Email Tracking Tools

You will need to track every single email or campaign that you send out. The reason, why is to understand which emails get clicks and responses versus ones that don't.

Here's a couple of options that I recommend below:

Streak for Gmail
Pricing: Pro Version $49 per month

Receive a notification when your proposal is viewed, and you'll know exactly when to follow up. Know if your email is read and not responded to, or never reaches the recipient. Streak offers many other features besides tracking so it's worth reviewing further.

Track everything and always have context Information about your pipelines, contacts, and tasks directly in your inbox and pocket.

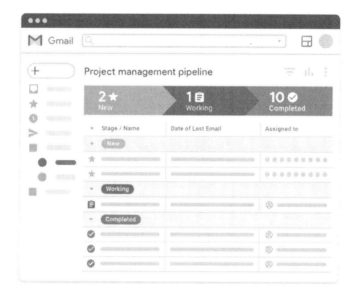

You can also use Streak to track applicants through the hiring process (CRM).

Track your applicants where you talk to them – in your email. Streak builds on your

22

existing email habits to create an easy and efficient experience.

Use One Efficient System Stop the endless switching from email to an external ATS and then back again. Streak users never BCC, forward, or copy and paste.

Familiar Design Work with the program you're already comfortable using – Gmail.

Don't waste time trying to learn another new piece of software. Make onboarding new users fast and easy.

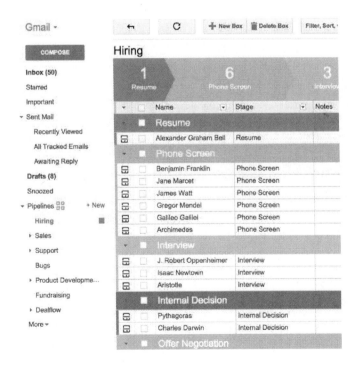

BananaTag for Gmail & Outlook
Pricing: Pro Version is $10 per month

They will send you a notification to your inbox when a contact opens your email or clicks a link. Emails tracked with Bananatag look no different to recipients and arrive from your address.

Capture all the Data:
Find out if leads are opening your emails and see which content, they're clicking on most.

Track Time:
Find out if employees are reading your content by measuring how long they spend in your emails.

Location & Device:
Type See how your content performs across different locations and on mobile and desktop.

Yesware for Gmail and Outlook
Pricing: Pro Version is $12 per month

Know who opens your emails and clicks on your links. It's simple and user-friendly to use. Email Tracking every moment counts when you are building relationships. Instantly see who's opening your emails, clicking on links or viewing attachments from your real-time activity feed.

MailTrack for Gmail and Outlook
Pricing: Pro Version is $4.99 per month

See in your mailbox if your emails have been opened. Again, is another one that's simple and easy to use.

Email Activity:
See in your mailbox if your emails have been opened.

Real-time Notifications:
Receive real-time notification pop-ups when your emails are opened.
Your Data is Secure:
The software is privacy compliant and will never share data with 3rd parties. Your company may have IT that is concerned by

third-party apps – this this might be a good option.

Contact Monkey for Gmail and Outlook
Pricing: Pro Version is $10 per month

See who's opening your email. Right from your inbox. Gather insights from email analytics and refine your internal communications strategy.

Track opens, clicks, survey responses, locations, and more! Analyze individual or overall campaign results to identify your most engaged employees, departments, or offices.

HubSpot for Gmail and Outlook
Pricing: Starter Version is $50 per month

Know the second a lead opens an email, send a perfectly timed follow-up, and close deals faster than ever. With email tracking, you get a desktop notification the second a prospect opens your email and clicks a link inside.

Take the time to personalize your outreach after a lead engages with your emails, and continue to automate outreach to prospects who don't.

You'll spend less time chasing cold prospects and more time closing warm leads.

Tip: I recommend using Bitly within your email to track if the candidates are linking on any links that you are sharing – including the job description.

Final thoughts
Bringing it all together. I recommend testing out a few of these tools before you decide on a final solution. The two that I recommend would be Streak and Mailtrack just because I've had success with both in the past with a limited budget.

Email Deliverability Tools

Have you ever sent a fantastic recruiter email to a passive candidate never to hear anything back?

Writing a well thought out email that calls out the candidate experience and interest takes a lot of time and effort for a recruiter.

Maybe this thought crossed your mind while waiting patiently for a response? Maybe your emails are being sent directly to the dreaded spam folder or maybe your email never got delivered at all?

There's a lot of good reasons for why it makes sense to test out your email deliverability when sending a recruiter message.

Here's some reasons why it makes sense to test your email deliverability:
- Before you start a sourcing email campaign.
- If you are using automation tools.
- If you are not getting a low response rate back from emails.
- If you get a response saying they never got your email message etc.

- Maybe you have a general hunch that this is the reason.

Unfortunately, on top of these reasons sometimes passive candidates do get annoyed by the amount of recruiter emails that they do receive. You could send the most well thought out message and the recipient still could consider a cold email as spam. Google and other email services will penalize you for getting sent to the spam folder over and over.

I can't stress this enough. Take the time to send a well throughout email template. Don't send the same message to every lead. You may not realize it – but you might be the one considered spamming. Below are the tools that I recommend reviewing further.

1. Mail-Tester (Basic)
Is a free tool that analyzes your email scores. It's a less advanced version that allows you to send up to 3 email messages per day for free. You just go to their website and copy the email address generated for you. Then you send your email to this address and you get a report.

You will receive a score (0-10) and 10 being the best. If you are receiving a score of 5-6 then you should probably take action and invest in an email tool. This is great for independent recruiters who don't want to have a large budget to assess this problem. You can take this information and invest later down the line.

2. Spam Check from PostMark (Basic)
This is a free tool to check your overall email deliverability. This tool will give you a basic score for you to help analyze what's happening with your emails. Important: the lower score you get here, the better. Anything close to 5 or higher will be most probably automatically marked as spam by your prospects' email providers.

Have you ever wanted to process the spam score of incoming or outgoing email messages, but didn't want the hassle of managing SpamAssassin? Now you can use our lightweight JSON API and instantly integrate spam score processing in your app. This service is provided for free from Postmark, the transactional email service for web apps.

3. GlockApps (Advanced)

If you are on a mid to large scale recruiting team. It makes sense to invest in a well-developed tool that can cover all your bases.

This tool has several advanced features that cover: inbox checkers, reputation checks, bounce analytics, template editors and overall content analysis. I would recommend getting a demo of this tool to see and understand all its benefits.

On average 51% of emails never reach the inbox! So where do they go? 26% go to spam or junk folders and 25% are never delivered.

The most common reasons are:
- Domain Reputation
- Authorization Fails
- IP Blacklisted
- Risky Content
- Being Marked as spam

Glockapps works with every major email hosting website including: Mac, Gmail, Outlook, Yahoo, Hotmail and many others.

4. MailGun (Large Scale)
I was recommended this tool by my developer friend. This one is more advanced

and would be used to support a small recruiting agency with their email needs.

Your deliverability is affected by a multitude of factors such as your industry, sending volume, traffic segmentation, and sender reputation. It makes sense to invest in a large-scale tool if you have a team of recruiters that rely heavily on email outreach.

When you sign up for an account you will be assigned an account manager. They will assess the current state of your email strategy and infrastructure and advise you on how to build out a deliverability strategy custom to your business.

Here's what MailGun Offers:
- Deliverability and recipient engagement management.
- Managed IP warmup ensures the health of your IP.
- Email tracking and testing consulting.
- Email reputation and deliverability reports.

Chapter 2: Follow the Best Outreach Practices

Being able to determine the best methods of reaching and communicating with candidates can mean the difference between successfully engaging versus missing the mark entirely.

Just as each target audience has similar interests and preferred social media platforms, they likely favor a form of communication as well.

The following chapters will discuss formatting for the various modes of messaging, including email, InMail, and text; but despite those components, the number one goal is getting their attention.

Prompt Them to Engage Immediately
At the time of this writing, we are experiencing a worker shortage, so naturally, the most talented professionals in most industries are being invited to consider new positions. For the recipients, that could equate to anywhere from fifteen to thirty-five messages in a single day.

Unless those messages are personalized and void of common template styles or canned messages, most (if not all) will be ignored.

Bottom line, you must get their attention. Once you get to know your target audience, you will be able to surmise what their interests, hopes, and fears are and use that to your advantage.

Construct a message that will convey genuine empathy and understanding of the candidate and how you can satisfy their needs rather than addressing your own needs (i.e. - filling a position for your client).

Initially, the primary goal is to pique their interest and entice them to read your message. By first making a human connection you can begin building a relationship and the rest will follow suit. Remember, you want to lure them in gradually rather than risk them turning the other way.

Follow Best Practices
Now comes the moment of truth and hopefully clarity as to why you must understand the role as well as the individual, you're interested in.

Next is structuring the outreach message in a way that piques their interest, makes them feel as though you care, and compose a message that resonates with them so they respond.

The Role
With an understanding of the role, you'll have the ability to describe the duties and make it interesting and attractive to your audience.

The Individual
Being familiar with the individual's background, transferable skills, and interests, your cognizance will enable you to reach out with familiarity and a sense of awareness.

Create a Message that Triggers a Response
We all like feeling understood and acknowledged. This is where you create an outreach message that "speaks" to them on a personal level. On average most emails will get viewed for less than 20-30 seconds.

Outreach Message Format

Structuring a format will save you time and help you structure the key points of your message.

Cut to the main points
State your intent in a way that peaks the individual's curiosity.

Make a connection
Within the message, share how/where you discovered them, a tidbit of unique or interesting information on what you learned about them, and reason for contacting them.

Explain the opportunity
Share a brief explanation about the job opportunity, including title and duties. Limit this to two sentences or less. Remember, the goal is to spark interaction.

Highlight the benefits
Clarify that you have their interests at heart. How would the opportunity benefit them? Keep in mind, they don't know you, so you must consider trust (and the lack thereof). Make it attractive and gently invite them to respond.

Call to Action

Suggest a brief phone call, zoom meeting, or at the very least, a reply to let you know they're not interested.

Share a part of yourself
Instead of merely closing with your name, include a link to your website, social media or company profile. After all, you shared what you know about them, so allow them to learn about you, too. Trust goes both ways, so "keep it real" to create the foundation of a good professional relationship.

Once you've drafted the message following this format, review before sending it. This is your opportunity to make that great first impression while capturing their attention through personalization and motivating them to respond.

Even if they fail to respond
I wouldn't immediately, get discouraged. This doesn't necessarily indicate there's no interest, rather they are probably busy much like everyone else. We'll also discuss protocols for follow-up messaging a bit later. On average it takes me 4-6 outreaches to connect with a passive lead.

Most everyone has an email address and people generally check their inboxes at least once a day. On the other hand, InMail can be costly and isn't ideal in every sourcing situation.

Then there's the option of texting, which is not recommended for cold-calling. Even when communication lines are opened, texting still might be perceived as too personal. Still, each method has advantages and disadvantages and timing plays a role in the process.

Email
Reaching out to candidates via email is one of the best options. For starters, it's basically free (unlike InMail) and when done correctly, it is very effective. Also, email services offer spam filtering whereas InMail does not.

InMail
InMail is specific to the LinkedIn platform and an excellent way to connect with both passive and active candidates directly. While there is a free version available to LinkedIn members, investing in a recruiter subscription will prove useful.

Text Message

Reaching out to candidates via text is not typically recommended, especially when cold- calling. However, when corresponding with candidates whom you've established communications with, ask how they prefer to receive updates and follow up messages from you.

Proper Timing
There are no hard and fast rules for determining the best time to message candidates, as it is highly dependent on your target audience. However, here are a few suggestions based on statistics:

Email Timing

Early morning or evening messages are opened more quickly than those sent mid-day.

Reaching out to candidates on the weekends may be off-putting, but if you're willing to take the risk, weekend emails present less competition.

The open ratio on emails sent Monday through Friday are even, but Thursday seems to offer a slightly higher open rate. (Source: LinkedIn.com)

It's Important to Note [Time Zones]
As with most marketing strategies, you're probably focusing on a target audience. If your audience lives in varying time zones, schedule your emails based on the time zone of the majority.

Best Day to Send an Email

Tuesday by far is the best day to send out an email. People are generally are motivated to start there week and are more engaged when it comes to reading emails.

Most Popular Times According to Statistics

The absolute most popular time for emails to be read is between 10 am and 11 am, with 10 being ideal. (Source: Getresponses.com)

Then, the next most popular time is a longer span of time, which ranges from 8 pm to midnight. Whether this is because many are in the habit of checking and responding to messages before going to bed or for those individuals who tend to be night owls, a large majority of emails are received and clicked on in the evening.

Coming in as the third most popular time of day for checking emails is 2 pm. For many, this is likely when some are finishing up their work day and routinely do this to wrap things up, or perhaps it's for those individuals that experience the all-too-common afternoon slump and tackle a task that requires less thought.

Let's not forget about those early birds who start their day before getting out of bed.

Statistics indicate that approximately 50% of people start their day this way, which is why 6 am seems to be yet another popular time for reaching emails.

Test Your Key Audience
You can also use the suggested guidelines as a foundation for testing your audience, scheduling them at the same time throughout the week. The results will also let you know which days of the week your audience is the most engaged.

According to a six-month study of 4 billion emails conducted by GetResponse, messages sent Monday through Friday were opened much more frequently than weekends. And, of the weekdays, Tuesday was a slightly more popular day. Then, in addition to the most popular days, you might also consider testing times of year. The key is starting and tweaking as you go.

Of course, it would be great if the collected data was clear cut and held true for everyone, but even the massive amounts of data available can't accurately do that. Why? Because audiences' habits vary based on interests, professions, age, and so on.

Get More Out of Your Emails
Compiling data on your audience is essential, albeit time-consuming and a bit daunting, especially if you're just building your email marketing skills. With the right tools and techniques, you'll be able to make the most of every email you send, ensuring that you get the most opens, clicks, and results from each campaign.

InMail Timing:

A major advantage to connecting with candidates via InMail is that LinkedIn is a prime platform for professionals to connect and obviously motivated candidates are frequently checking their inbox.

InMail open rates are higher during mid-morning (9am-10am). Apart from Saturday, your message is likely to be seen and responded to. Based on LinkedIn statistics,

Saturdays have a 16% reduction in responses. (Source: LinkedIn.com)

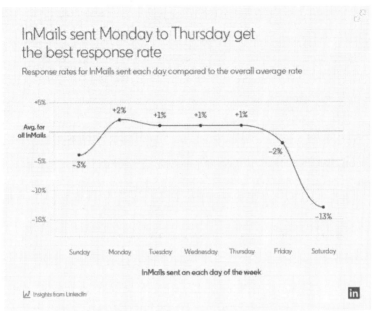

(Source: LinkedIn.com)

InMail Length Matters

In this technological-based world we live in, the average attention span is gradually decreasing. As of 2021, it is estimated that individuals 24 years old and younger, known as Gen Z have an 8-second attention span while Millennials, ages 25-40 can focus for an average of 11-seconds.

InMails that are short and concise, consisting of 400 characters or less, receive responses up to 41% more than longer messages.

This isn't to say that longer messages don't do well, and depending on both the correspondence and your targeted talent pool, an extremely brief message simply isn't helpful.

The fact is, currently only 10% of InMail messages fall into the extra short category, but that "to-the-point" approach is effective especially for the passive and/or extremely busy candidates.

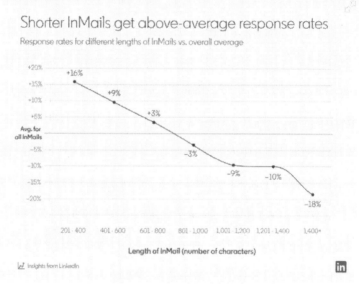

(Source: LinkedIn.com)

Texting Timing:

Just to reiterate, texting is the most personal. Therefore, if you text candidates, it's recommended that you limit texting to weekdays between 8am and 5pm (candidate's time zone).

Ultimately, you're setting a precedent and if you text on the weekends or late evening, then the individual will feel inclined to do the same with the expectation of an immediate response.

Undeniably, texting has become a popular form of communication personally and professionally. While it does open new options for recruiters to connect with candidates, it's not appropriate for all forms of communication.

For example, discussing sensitive topics such as salary should be done through a phone conversation or email.

Chapter 3: Get Their Attention

Putting in the effort to customize messages may seem too time consuming, with all the other responsibilities you have on your plate.

However, when you follow the recommended steps, it will get easier with practice. And, rest assured, sending an authentic, personalized message to each candidate will inevitably increase the response rate.

Your goal should be to create a stellar candidate experience for every applicant. That means you can't throw candidates into a cookie cutter process and expect them to feel valued and appreciated. Tailor your recruiting email templates to the individual, adding personal details and touches when possible.

Crafting a Subject Line

The goal here is to build an immediate connection with the candidate so he or she will read the message; and that starts with a spectacular subject line.

64% of email recipients make a decision to open emails based on subject lines. So even though you should focus on creating the copy and imagery of your recruiting email template, you shouldn't undermine the importance of a great subject line.

It's time to toss aside those generic subject lines such as Name, Title, or Company. Not only are they merely factual details, they lack any appeal or personalization whatsoever. While these may work for individuals desperately searching for a job, that's likely not the type of candidate you're interested in.

Instead, create something that is enticing, which is much easier when you have a bit of insight on the candidate's personality, interests, motivators, and so on.

Tried and True Examples Include:
- Following up on my call
- We connected a month back
- Just left a voicemail
- Trying to connect
- I was referred to you [etc.], and why you should chat with me

Examples for Gaining Curiosity:

- Company Name + This might just be your dream job...
- Perfect role for a [job title] with your qualifications
- Interested in a conversation about advancing your career?
- Looking for an excellent [job title] and would like to connect
- [Name] I'm Building an Avengers Marketing Team
- Let me introduce you to a better opportunity, [Name]
- Let me introduce you to a better opportunity, [Name]
- Want to grab a virtual coffee with me next week?

Using the company's name
- Company name: Your future job is here
- Hey (First name), have you already heard of (Company name)?
- Still enjoy getting up on a morning for (Company name), (First name)?
- Front-end Developer at (Company name) (USA, full-time, remote work)
- Greetings from (Company name)! – (Job title) Opportunities
- (Company name) The engineering team in Warsaw welcomes (First name)

- (First name), a quick note in regard to a Software Engineer role at (Company name)

"New opportunity" or a "Dream Job"
- A conversation about the future!
- Are you currently happy with your employer/ position?
- A Job that will change your world – Click here
- Have you heard about our new opportunity?

Skills- or Job Title-Based Subject Lines
- Software Engineer Opening – Salaried in Austin!
- Java Heaven! > or Compliance Heaven! > Their Greatest skill and then the word Heaven! and then the > sign

Creative Examples
- (Target's job function) + (Target's hobby or another non-work data point) = Your next job?
- Looking for software talent, I have found you, (First name). 🖤

- Let's build the technologies of tomorrow with rolling stock development!
- We Need to Talk (about your boring job)

(Source: Indeed.com)

Keep the subject line short, preferably less than nine words. Also, steer clear of using all CAPS, and words or phrases such as earn $, opportunity, free, money, or assistance that may trigger spam filters.

Most smartphones only display five or six words of a subject line. Because 41% of today's emails are opened on mobile devices, it's crucial to keep your subject lines crisp.

Basically, word the subject line in a way that will serve the candidate, rather than how they can serve you or the company.

Offer a Personalized Introduction
The introduction should convey key details about you (name, company, and title), your credentials, and an explanation of why you're talking to them.
With that established, next you want to show you're genuinely interested and

devoted some time to learn a few interesting details about them.

It's not difficult to learn about someone's hobbies and interests via personal blogs or social profiles. In order not to seem "creepy," try to link this with something associated with the company for which you're hiring.

For example: Do you still attend hacker conferences? (Company name) developers have their own local team.

Use "Praise" as a Sourcing Tactic

Next, explain what prompted you to reach out and where you found the information. Maybe it was a noted achievement they listed on their LinkedIn or GitHub profile, or perhaps their professional experience made them stand out above the rest.

Then, be sure to get right to the point and provide a brief overview about the available position and share specifics about the company's culture. If applicable, include a link to the company website, which can be helpful, especially for a new or small company.

Also, by including the link, you avoid a lengthy message and information overload.

Focus on them and not you!
This is the most common mistake I see even seasoned recruiters make. The email is not about but rather about them.

Don't tell them what you can do but what you can do for them. The more value you can provide in your emails, the more they're likely to engage. As a result, it'll be much easier to get them to take the actions you want them to take.

Finally, end the message with an offer to discuss the position further, suggesting a date and time frame for the meeting.

Chapter 4: The Follow Up

Following up with candidates is yet another critical step. The longer you wait to send an important follow-up email or application status update, the more time you're allowing for another employer to swoop in and hire your candidate. Be prompt with your email correspondence and stick to any timelines you set for yourself.

Although this step is often dismissed by recruiters, it should apply to all candidates. From following up with non- responsive candidates to communicating with the successful candidates and even thanking the unsuccessful ones for their time.

Basically, failure to follow up with every lead may result in that individual developing a negative perception about you, the recruiter, as well as the hiring company. Rather, when you take on the mindset of treating all candidates like valued clients, you avoid burning bridges and destroying Candidate-Recruiter relationships, as future opportunities may present a perfect match.

For the purposes of this book, we'll focus on the best practices for following up with non-responsive candidates.

Following Up with Non-Responsive Candidates

First and foremost, following up with non-responsive candidates will increase your chances of getting a reply. This next (crucial) step is one way to ensure you stand out from other recruiters. Why?

The most common reasons why some recruiters may avoid following up include:

- Not wanting to seem pushy or annoying.

- Feeling rejected. That's right, a large majority of recruiters perceive the initial lack of response as disinterest and give up.

- Giving up too soon.

However, everyone is busy and just maybe your initial message was missed or forgotten. Therefore, view the follow up email as another opportunity to grab their attention.

Why Follow up Emails are Important

While it's quite possible that your follow up email(s) may be more triggering, it's more likely that timing played a role. According to research, approximately 90% of emails are opened and replied to on the day they are received, whereas that percentage drops down to 3% after twenty-four hours. With, your follow-up emails increase the chances of a reply.

The Follow Up Timeframe

Creating a follow up timeline that works for you will ensure you maintain consistency as well as give the candidates a nudge, without being irritating.

Of course, there are no hard and fast rules and it's highly recommended that you do a bit of testing on your own. In general, a follow up schedule should look something like this:

1st Follow up: 1-2 days after initial email
2nd Follow up: 3-4 days after initial email
3rd Follow up: 7-14 days after initial email

Typically, if a passive candidate hasn't responded after a month of follow up emails, it's likely you won't hear from them at all.

Set a Goal for Each Campaign:

Experienced recruiters have message goals. When I was first starting out, I would not track my emails. By not doing that I wasn't able to set goals for myself.

Goal #1 Get a response (even if it's a no)
Goal #2 Improve the call to action
Goal #3 Get the lead on the phone
Goal #4 Set a goal for the number of clicks

Closing the Loop with Non- Responsive Candidates

Sending a "goodbye" or "break-up" email to candidates is a great way to close the loop. Even when you're dealing with an unresponsive candidate, it's good practice to say goodbye. Not only does this give you one more chance to spark their attention, it protects your professional reputation and company brand.

This style of email triggers the "FOMO" (fear of missing out) response and essentially puts the ball in their court. Statistics show that 22.5% of replies gained from these last-minute attempts are from those final "goodbye" messages.

When creating a goodbye email, it should contain the following three components.

Let them know you have attempted to reach them several times, but they have not responded to your messages.

Make sure they know this is your last attempt to reach them.

Include your contact information in the event they decide to reach out to you in the future.

You may want to take it a step further by providing a few enticing highlights of what they're missing out on.

Follow Up Dos and Don'ts
Although we tend to focus on finding and hiring the top talent, all candidates deserve (and most expect) a response, just as they're expected to follow up after an interview.

Let's look at what you should DO whether trying to get a non-responsive candidate to reply or interacting with receptive candidates.

Keep the message short and to the point
Whether you include a copy of the previous email or highlight an aspect that serves as a reminder, keep your messages short and concise.

Maintain a single email thread

By maintaining a single thread of email communication with each candidate, it allows you to keep candidate information organized and serves as a refresher for the candidate.

Analyze your data on a regular basis

Take full advantage of your digital tools and the collected data. This information will help you gain invaluable insight so you can tweak content and subject lines as well as determine what produces the best response rates.

Use multiple channels

If a candidate isn't responsive to an email or InMail, yet you see activity elsewhere, consider another type of outreach. Something as simple as commenting on a Facebook or LinkedIn post may prompt a reply. It all boils down to determining where they spend more time in the digital world.

In the following section, we'll share some things you should NOT DO when following up with candidates.

Don't be lazy

While you need to reference your initial email message, you should also include fresh content, even if it's a single sentence. Resending the same message makes you appear lazy.

Do not follow up more than a few times
If a candidate does not respond after 3-4 follow up attempts, you should close the loop and stop. The last thing you want is to be a nuisance.

Do not apologize
Refrain from using apologetic phrases like "I don't want to be a bother" "I apologize" or "I'm sorry." You should never apologize for trying to make them aware of a potentially great opportunity.

Choosing your words carefully
Use "you", "you're", "you could" in your emails. Instead of sending look at ME emails. Effective cold emails are not self-focused.

Avoid using buzz words
A message shouldn't be filled with buzzwords or copy and pasting. Instead, messages should have a casual conversational tone.

Buzz word terms include:
- Fast leader

- Proven track record
- Hardworking
- Highly motivated
- Works well under pressure

When constructing a follow up email, do your best to create a "hook" subject line and include an irresistible call-to-action. Additionally, include something of value.

For example, instead of a nonchalant 'just following up' add 'just following up to hear your thoughts on [prior email subject].

Finally, creating a clear call to action. Writing a message that is unclear won't encourage the lead to respond back.

Here's how to set a clear call to action:
- I didn't ask a question they had to respond to.
- Tell them what to do if they were interested.
- Push them towards a meeting.
- How to find out more information.
- How to make immediate contact.

Sample #1

[Hi Name]

[Hi Name]
I reached out to you last week, but I can't imagine how busy you are. I would still like to chat with you regarding our open senior engineering positions.

Are you free for a 15 min chat this week?

Sample #2

[Hi Name]
I thought I'd send you one last email.

We are trying to fill a brilliant tech role at a fantastic company and would love to have a chat with you about it.

Just hit reply if you would like to know more about this team. I am sure it would be a great next move in your career.

Sample #3

Hi [candidate's name],

I hope this email finds you well. I know you applied to our [previous open position] back in [month or year], and while we went in a different direction then, we kept you top of mind.

A [position] just opened up at [organization's name], and I think you'd be a great fit.

I'd love to reconnect, discuss the role and hear about what you've been up to since we last spoke. Would you be available for a quick phone call on [date and time]?

I look forward to hearing from you soon.

Chapter 5: Write, Rinse, Repeat

Understanding how to capture candidates' attention in your emails is key. Of course, the subject line needs to grab their attention and compel them to open and read the email, then the body of the email needs to be short and to the point while conveying your message.

Whether your goal is to schedule an interview, follow up, or even offer the candidate a job, when you follow the techniques below, you'll experience higher open rates and the success of winning them over.

Focus on Calling out Uniqueness
This can include the name drop of a mutual connection, an industry-related post or even a unique (or silly) video they shared on social media.

Oftentimes, a recruiter's initial outreach revolves around explaining how they discovered the candidate (i.e. LinkedIn, Facebook, etc.) but -- since most recruiters send the same canned messages -- they are often flagged as spam for saying something like, "Hey, I found you on LinkedIn."

So, while saying where you found the candidate can certainly help validate the connection, it's best to focus on a unique aspect or a specific eye-catching skill about the candidate.

Your Initial Goal is to entice not Sell
The first email should be enticing, focused on praising them for their accomplishments, pointing out a unique aspect, or finding common ground via shared connections or interests. Bottom line, the goal is to hook them into wanting to learn more!

A high-level candidate receives thousands of recruiter messages, hence why your message needs to stand out and be alluring enough to make them respond based on your CTA, whether that's to connect over the phone, on Zoom, etc.

Here's what your message should entail:
- Tell who you work for
- Establish credibility
- How can you help me?
- What's the main purpose of this message?

You Are the Artist

Indicative of the book title, Art of the Recruiter Message, it is an artform when it comes to understanding how to reach out to candidates online.

First Email/Message should be funny/catchy/unique.

Second Email/Message should follow up and then sell the team/role/specific reason.

Third & Fourth Email/Message should be more follow up for subsequent responses.

The Main Point of the Message Should Address a Candidates "WHY"

When you construct your message around the candidate's interest, you're more likely to get a response. Consider the reasons why someone might be searching for a new job or career opportunity.

Examples include:
- Career advancement
- Schedule flexibility
- Being promoted (i.e. from senior level to a managerial position)
- Opportunity to use cutting edge technology

- Location/Remote work (this is extremely important)
- Higher salary and/or better benefits

Another approach is including perks that might appeal to the candidate if the role for which you're hiring has such attributes.

For instance, an opportunity for mentorship, on the job training and the potential to grow within a field. Perhaps the hiring company is committed to providing their team various opportunities that enrich the individuals on a personal level as well as increase their professional value to the company.

If a company is experiencing a lot of growth, be sure to include that as it conveys stability and future opportunities. It can also be effective to point out a team member's recent achievements. If a recent hire made an impressive transition, point it out (We recently had a former Uber manager join our team.)

Most candidates are looking for much more than a paycheck. They want to work in an environment where they can contribute and with a company that takes time to know their employees.

You can accomplish a good image by including the hiring manager's email in your correspondence and explaining that they are growing their team. After that, ask the hiring manager to follow up by email. It's great when HMs reach out to the candidates. Rather than a boring, sales-focused recruiter.

Develop Reusable Message Formats
In the average recruiter's work week, 13 hours are spent sourcing for one position.

Due to the vast number of tasks recruiters are expected to accomplish, that is quite a bit of time, which is why it is so important to create formats for messages that can be customized and reused again and again.

Having a go-to format eliminates the risk of forgetting to mention important details, in addition to improving the process. Of course, you don't want to fall into the trap of sending "canned" messages, so take the time to personalize it. While this may seem time consuming, it will be worth it in the end.

Cold Email Templates

Recruiters are quickly recognizing that "quality over quantity" is the best solution when reaching out to a lead online.

Sending bulk emails that are not personalized don't work in this market. Taking the time to research and personalize will be vital for your success.

Contacting potential candidates for the first time is basically your chance to make a great first impression. When you send them your first email, let them know you researched their accomplishments to grab their attention.

Follow these steps when writing cold email messages:

Explain why they would specifically be a great fit at [company name]. Remember, it is not about you - it is all about them!

Avoid pushing for a phone call at first. Email or LinkedIn is preferable. If you wish to call, provide the option, but do not insist.

Include the name of the company you represent and its industry. Avoid secrecy, as it decreases my interest in responding.

Provide details about the company's operations and achievements, avoiding buzzwords and generic statements.

Specify the stage of the company, the role being offered, its reporting structure, and its challenges.

Avoid offering irrelevant praise, and be clear about how you found them.

Specify the location of the opportunity, and avoid making assumptions about my willingness to relocate.

Provide specific information about compensation.

Tip: Be Empathic & Encouraging
The following template is a great option for reaching out to a candidate for the first time. This template grabs the reader's attention on a personal level, which helps warm them up.

Plus, it effectively introduces the writer (you), further nurturing a strong professional connection.

Sample #1

Subject Line: Interested in joining [Company Name] as the new [job title]?

Hi [Name],

This is [your name/title] with [company name]. I was doing a search in [specific niche/skill set] and your name came up multiple times in my quest for talent.

[Company] is looking to hire someone with your [specific skill set]. I thought you might be interested; or since you have a lot of connections, perhaps you know someone who is looking to make a move.

Would love the chance to connect over a phone call to discuss this further.

Are you available this Thursday?

[Name]

Tip: Emphasize a Shared Connection

These two templates focus on emphasizing a shared connection. By simply using that mutual friend's name, you're being re-categorized in their mind from "random stranger" to a personal acquaintance, and that's the first step in outreach.

Sample #2

Subject Line: [Name of Mutual Connection] suggested we connect

Hi [First Name],

[Your name] here. I'm from [Company Name] and during a conversation with [Name of mutual friend] about hiring a [job title], I also
learned that we're all big [college sport/activity] enthusiasts!

[Company Name] is looking for a talented [job title] and I thought this would be a great career move for you.

Would you have time for a brief chat this Friday?

Tip: If the individual's personal interests align with the company's culture, another approach would be to mention something non-related:

Sample #3

Hi [First name],

[Your Name] here. I'm from [Company Name] and during a conversation with [Name of mutual friend] about hiring a [job title] I also learned that we're all big college enthusiasts!

We both attended the same college and we're fans of the football team. The [Company] has a remarkable sales team, and with your competitive spirit I think your skills would make a great addition.

If you'd like to learn more, let's schedule a call. Are you available this Wednesday?

In this approach, you could also include a relevant video snippet or image depicting the company's football [or applicable activity]. This implements the power of visuals and increases the chances of grabbing the recipient's attention.

Lastly, avoid the temptation of bloating the message with company details, as this will decrease the chance of a reply and the reader will perceive it as diverting your attention away from him or her. The following approach will effectively address any concerns.

Draw a Parallel between the Recipient and Industry

When approaching a passive candidate, it can be tricky. First, regardless of the details you've compiled about an individual from their social media and professional profiles, you ultimately don't know how they will truly respond. On top of that, if you're hiring for a new or small company, you may be concerned that they're not even familiar with the company or industry. In this case, the following approach may be useful.

Sample #4

Subject Line: Your [Project Name] on [Platform Name: i.e. GitHub & BitBucket] projects truly impressed me and my hiring manager [name drop]

Hi [First Name],

I'm [Your Name/Title] with [your company]. I saw your profile on [platform] and I was impressed by your [Project Name] post! It certainly received a lot of rep-stars on GitHub.

I head up talent acquisition on behalf of [Client Company]. They are looking for a [job title] who is both skilled and passionate in the field.

After seeing your achievements and recent project. I think this would resonate with my [Client Company].

If this interests you, perhaps we could discuss it more in detail.

I look forward to hearing from you soon!

Tip: Remember, your goal is to entice them to make that initial connection.

Consider their interests, as well as tonalities. And while words like team, ninja, power, driven, or relentless focus words can be appealing to some, these same words may deter a female gender applicant from applying.

Sample #5

Hi [First Name],
I came across your profile on [platform] and found your professional achievements to be astounding, including: [list examples].

I was wondering if you would be open to learning more about what we're doing at [company]. At our [company] we are working on [list examples].

If this interests you, please contact me. Kind regards,

[Name]

Grab their attention with a funny or catchy subject line.

In the sea of thousands of emails received by top candidates, the subject line can often determine whether your email is ignored or opened.

Sample #6

Subject line: Wait! What time are you reading this email?

Hey [First Name],

If you're reading this email late evening or on the weekend, perhaps you're ready for a career move? Maybe you'd love something that is challenging, offers flexible hours, and where you can be a part of a team that knows how to achieve goals but still have fun in the process.

[Your Name] here. I'm with [Company]. We're hiring for [job title] and need intelligent, fun people to join us. I understand if you're not ready to make a move from your current position with [Company], but your skills and interests certainly align with what we're looking for!

Let me know if you're available for a quick chat so I can share more details.

Look forward to hearing from you soon!

"Keep It Simple"
KISS, an acronym coined by the U.S. Navy in the 1960s, meaning "Keep it simple, stupid" is important, but when it comes to Cold Email Recruiting, keeping it simple and SHORT is not only applicable, it's crucial.

If you want high response rates, then your initial emails need to be clear, concise, and easy to understand.

For instance, if you're recruiting for an industry that you're very knowledgeable about, it's likely you take certain details for granted or perhaps even use industry-specific jargon. But you should not assume the candidates you want to engage with know the industry in the same capacity as you.

Remember, it's important that your emails are informative, not impressive. Stay away from buzzwords and opt easy-to-digest phrasing instead of long, complex terms. Your goal is not to be clever, it's to connect with a talented candidate whom you don't truly know.

According to research, emails that are simply written, equivalent to a 3rd grade reading level will typically have more responses.

Sample #7

Hi [First Name],

This is [Your Name] with [Company]!

I noticed your extensive background in [Industry]. [Client Company Name] is looking to add a [Role] and I believe the opportunity could help advance your skills in [example]. Our company has been given the green light to build out a new team focused on this cutting- edge technology.

Let's have a conversation to go over the prospect in more detail.

Let me know if you're available this week for a call.

Focus on The Candidate's Benefits

In addition to keeping, it short and simple, don't forget the important rule of WIIFM (What's in it for me?) So often, recruiters count on the mere job opportunity being interesting, but if the outreach message is more focused on how the company will benefit, rather than what's in it for the candidate, they're not going to care, much less respond.

So, put yourself in the shoes of the candidate and address the WIIFM aspect.

Will your email prompt the response of "so what" or will it peak their interest enough to send you a reply in hopes of learning more?

Again, your research into the target audience will be beneficial here. For example, if you are targeting millennials, then most likely they place high value on a business that is involved in community outreach, but also want X amount in salary etc.

On the other hand, if you're targeting centennials (aka Gen. Z) then working for a business that values a healthy work-life balance and is open to scheduling flexibility is a key factor.

Likewise, you want to explain the unique values your client company offers versus the competition.

Sample #8

Hi [First Name],

This is [Your name/title] and on behalf of [Client Company Name], we're seeking a [job title]. After reviewing your credentials on [platform], I think the offer would interest you. Why?

Here are 3 reasons:

- ✓ Impressive benefits package, including (i.e. childcare, student loan assistance, life coaching, and so on.)
- ✓ Advancement opportunities including in mentorship.

- ✓ A competitive salary structure that includes commissions.

How about a call tomorrow afternoon, so I can share more details?

Tip: Make scheduling a call your primary goal. Always include a call-to-action that provides clear instructions.

Sample #9

Hi [First Name],

I was reading through your [portfolio, Facebook page, blog, or work] and have a few ideas you might find interesting.

I realize with your skills and professional background, you probably receive a lot of similar emails, but I think this one may be more relevant for you.

In my experience, it's important to match not only the best talent to the position, I like to ensure company/employee values and goals align with each other.

While I recognize that the timing of my email may or may not be ideal for you, I can't pass up the chance to have a conversation with you, to see if this opportunity is of any interest.

Would you prefer to connect via phone call or zoom?

Sample #10

Hi [name], I'm [name] and I found your website as I was perusing through the black hole of Twitter and [mutual connection] had great things to say about you. I saw that you're currently at [company], but wanted to reach out in case you're open to a new opportunity.

I'm looking to is hiring a content marketing manager with a starting salary of [salary] with equity options.

We just closed our series B of funding [link to announcement] and we're looking to develop our content playbook as a channel for user acquisition.

Our team would like to talk to you more and have you lead our content team to help us jump start those efforts. Would you like to learn more?

Sample #11

Hi [name], My (company) is growing their data science teams and both have interesting research areas so thought they could be a good fit.

They are a pharmaceutical company with a consumer health tracking app and most of their data science is around ingredient research and product development. This role would have an engineering and machine learning component like your current role at (company).

Would you be open to learning more over a call?

Sample #12

Hey [name], I've been networking with other finance startups in Brooklyn and your name and project kept coming in my searches.

I wanted to see if you might be open to networking for a possible career move at this time.

My start-up recently gained further funding we're looking at hiring a software manager to grow a new team.

You're experience and skills, particularly [insert skill], make you a terrific fit for what we're trying to do over at [Company].

I'd love to tell you a bit more about [Company], [role], and why I think you would love it!

Do you have time for a short call on Monday?

Sample #13

Hi [name], "Keep your goals away from the trolls" - knew I had to reach out after I read this on your twitter. :D

Might get this up as a motivational poster in the office! I must know where you found it! I saw that when you're not fighting trolls, you're a killer sales rep! Awesome work helping your team nail its targets last quarter, you guys are growing insanely fast...

I thought I'd reach out because we're building our sales team at [Company] and I think you'd be a great fit.

Do you have some time next week for a quick call to talk about the role?

Best, [Your Name]

Sample #14

Hi [name], While I was on your [professional networking site, personal website, etc.], I came across your [project or accomplishment] and just have to say, the work you're doing in [tech field] (and your passion behind it) is exactly what [company name] needs in a new [title of open role].

What do you say to grabbing coffee next week? We can chat more then and find out if it could be a match for you. Let me know if you're interested and I'll set something up.

Best, [Your name]

Tip: Strike a Balance
Regardless of how awesome your email outreach is, you know having an actual conversation with the candidate will be more effective in getting to the next stage. The previous sample was geared towards making the personalization subtle as well as informative.

Sometimes, it's all about striking a balance. In stating how you found their information, noting their achievements, and briefly mentioning the job opening, you demonstrate a genuine interest and avoid coming across as someone shady.

Sample #15

[Name],

I was really impressed by some of your work, which caught my eye on [website]. I dug a little deeper and found some of the awesome blogs you wrote at [company].

We currently have an opening for [job] at [company] and, based on your achievements, I think you'd be a really great fit!

If you're open to hearing more about it, feel free to grab some time on my calendar [calendar link] this week or next.

Regards,
[Name]

Warm Email Templates

Of course, as you build that go-to list of awesome candidates, there will be times when you already have a rapport from a previous connection. Rather than taking the name- dropping approach, captivate them with a personalized message.

Sample #1

Hi [First Name],

This is [your name]. I'm a recruiter with [Company]. We met last month to discuss your application for [position] at [Company].

During our conversation, you mentioned you had recently moved to the area. How do you like it so far?

Although another candidate was hired for that position, your uplifting attitude and impressive skill set were not forgotten.

Now, there is an opening for [role] with [company] that I think would be a great fit for your expertise and personality.

How about a call [date/time frame], so I can share more details with you?

Tip: Referrals are often the highest quality hires. If you have the opportunity, encourage others to share referrals with you. Be sure to provide them with the job details and the best way to contact you. Also, don't forget to ask for permission to use the referring person's name in your outreach. It's a great way to establish trust and build relationships with potential candidates.

Sample #2

Hi [First Name],

This is [Your Name/title] with [Company]. We have an opening for [job title] and [Referral Name] gave me your name.

The details provided on your [platform] profile is quite impressive. Your skills and experience combined with your involvement with business and community events, I think you might find this new role interesting.

[Company name] is always ready to scoop up great people and based on what

[Referral Name] shared, I would like to meet with you.

Is there any chance you are available [Date/time frame]?

Sample #3

I hope this email finds you well. We had reached out a while back regarding opportunities with a well-known technology company.

Obviously, things continue to go well at [CompanyName], but your name resurfaced in regards to a specific opportunity in which I thought might be of interest.

They have a strong track record with candidates that come from a similar background. I thought it made sense to reconnect given the specific nature of the search as we approach bonus season.

If you are interested in a chat to learn more, please let me know when would be a convenient time for you. Thank you again for your time. I look forward to hearing from you.

Sample 4#

Hi [First Name],

I hope this email finds you well. I know you applied to our [Previous Role] back in [Month or Year], and while [we went in a different direction then, or we paused our search because of the Covid-19 pandemic], we kept you top of mind.

A [Job Title] position just opened up at [your company] and given your [detail about the candidate], I think you'd be a great fit.

I'd love to reconnect, discuss the role and hear about what you've been up to since we last spoke. Would you be available for a quick phone call on [date/time]?

I hope you and your loved ones are safe and healthy, and I look forward to hearing from you soon.

Sample 5#

Hi [First Name],
[Contact's Name] gave me your email address — we [How you know the contact].

They speak very highly of you and your [Experience/Expertise].

I work for [Company's Name], and we're in the market for a [Job Title]. [Contact's Name] recommended you for the job and I think you'd be a great fit.

I'd love to learn more about you and tell you about the role. Are you free for a quick phone call [Date/Time]?

I hope you and your loved ones are safe and healthy and look forward to connecting. Best [name]

Sample 6#

Hi, [name]!

I hope you're doing well. You applied for [previous position] a few months ago. While it didn't work out, I have never stopped looking for an opportunity that would be a true fit for you—and I believe I found it.

[company] is actively hiring a [position]. You are an ideal candidate because of your

[previous experience]. You can view the complete job description [here].

You'll be excited to hear that [company] is a great place to work. It values a healthy work-life balance and offers educational opportunities so its employees can continue to expand their knowledge and skillsets.

I would love to speak with you about this position. Please use the [calendar link] to select a time for a quick chat in the next week.

InMail Templates

Connecting with candidates through InMail is a great choice. However, messaging passive candidates and getting noticed with this method can be tricky. Following are a few LinkedIn InMail Templates and tips that can help improve open and response rates.

Creating LinkedIn InMail Subject Lines

Like email, the InMail subject line should capture the recipient's attention by taking a personalized approach.

The following examples include subject lines for a referral, praise, and connecting a personal interest with the hiring company's culture.

[Mutual Connection Name] told me to connect with you.

Seeking [Skills] at [Company] [Location]

[Company Name] seeks nature-loving sales representatives

Keep it Short
Since your goal is to connect with the candidate, keep the body of the message under 100 words to respect the recipient's time.

The following template can be used if you're communicating with several candidates through InMail. From there, based on the candidate's personality and interests, as well as the available job, you can decide what to change. Your message should clearly state the company name, job title, and location preferences within the first title or paragraph.

Sample #1

Hi [First Name],

I can see you have a lot of solid experience in the [field] which immediately caught my eye.

I'm in the process of hiring for [job title] at [client industry]. With your background and current work, I felt the need to make an introduction.

I've actively pursuing a leader in the space and wanted to see if you would be open to talking further about an opportunity?

It would be great to get to know you better and tell you more about the position. Is [day and time] convenient for you?

[Name]

Grab Their Attention with Praise
Depending on the type of candidate you're looking for, flattery can be an effective approach. After all, if they've listed personal interests, accomplishments, most likely they enjoy the recognition it gains.

Sample #2

Hi [First Name],

I saw your publication on [topic] that won you multiple awards in our industry. Without question, you are an authority figure in that field, which is why I'm reaching out to you.

There's a leadership role in that industry opening at [Company Name] and I know that it could open new doors to advance your career.

I would love to share the details with you.

Does [day and time] work for you?

Look for a Referral Connection
Having a mutual connection can often be a great ice-breaker when reaching out to a candidate for the first time. While these are considered more of a "warm connection," it's still helpful to point out something specific about the candidate that you learned from their profile.

Sample #3

[Name]
I hope you had fun and safe new year.

Our connections at [Company Name] have some great things to say about you and your work and as it turns out.

We are a leading design-focused headhunting firm in NYC with clients like PayPal, Instagram and others in the best of tech.

We are working with some incredible firms with growing diverse teams and would love to work with you.

You come highly recommended and we are very impressed with your work at [candidate company name]. I am getting in touch to see if we can get on a call sometime to have a quick chat about your career goals.

Sample #4

Hi [First Name],

I recently had a conversation with [Referrer's Name], who mentioned your background in [industry].

It prompted me to review your LinkedIn and GitHub profiles and your expertise along with your dedication to community outreach makes me think you would find the open position of [job title] at [Company Name] very interesting.

Are you available to chat more about the details? If so, does [day and time] work for you?

I look forward to hearing from you!

Sample #5:

Hi [First Name],

We connected several months back on Twitter. I just saw your tweet about your recent vacation trip.

I have to say that I'm quite impressed with your skiing skills! :D

How long have you been skiing? I have taken it up last year and can't wait to glide over the snow the way you do.

I am looking for Front End developers like you for our client. They have a fledgling skiing club that really needs a pro skier like you. Also, the engineering team is looking for a new lead for the front-end team.

Would you be interested in a brief call to chat about the role sometime this week?

Sample #6

Hi [Name]
I just read your recent medium post about how yoga and meditation and how it's helped you in the creative process.

I am thoroughly impressed with your commitment to design and your out- of-the-box thought process. Your work at [current company] is impressive.

One of our clients is a trailblazing startup in NYC. As they've grown to more than 50 people in just two years, they are looking for someone to lead their design efforts. This is a leadership position where you would get to define their design roadmap for many years to come.

I think this would be a great role for you.

Would you be interested in having a brief chat about it sometime this week?

Sample #7

Hey [Name],
I hope you're having a great day! My name is [Your Name] and I'm a recruiter with [Company Name].

I came across your profile and was blown away by your skills and experience in data science.

I wanted to reach out and see if you might be interested in an exciting opportunity that we have available at our company. We're looking for a data scientist to join our team and work on some really cool projects that involve analyzing and interpreting data to solve complex business problems.

Now, I know you're probably receiving a ton of generic recruiting emails, so I wanted to make this one a little more fun and unique. So, here's a little riddle for you: What has a head and a tail, but no body? (Answer at the end!)

If this opportunity sounds like something you might be interested in, I'd love to chat with you more and see if it's a good fit. Just let me know if you're free to talk at your convenience and we'll set something up.

Looking forward to hearing from you!
[Your Name]

P.S. The answer to the riddle is a coin! (I hope you didn't spend too much time trying to solve it!)

Tip: Never Forget the Call to Action Regardless of how great your InMail message is, if you fail to include a "Call to action," any sense of urgency is missed. Whether you choose to use a gentle nudge like 'Looking forward to hearing from you," or suggest a date and time, at the end of every message, it's important to provide clear instructions of what the reader should do next.

Scarcity or FOMO
Your message needs to evoke an emotion in your prospect's mind. The emotion that I've seen usually performs well in cold

templates is the fear of missing out, or FOMO.

As recruiters, you can generate a sense of scarcity or FOMO that moves them to action. However, you cannot be too brazen about it but subtly hint that they don't want to miss out on what you are offering.

Follow Up Email Templates
Follow up emails are crucial in helping you close the deal. The follow up message doesn't need to be long or difficult. Check out the following examples.

Short and Direct
Unlike the initial email when you need to introduce yourself and grab the candidate's attention, the goal of the follow up email is to refresh their memory and get them to respond.

Don't get discouraged if your first follow up email doesn't prompt a response. According to statistics it can take between 3 and 4 follow up emails. Keeping it short and direct can be quite effective.

8-10 seconds is the average attention span a person gives to one task

Whether you're trying to break through the noise and capture the attention of your candidates or prospects, the key is to be as concise as possible.

Studies have shown that emails with 75 to 100 words have the highest response rate. You may want to share a lot of information in your cold recruiting emails, but recipients might not have the time for all of it.

Sample #1

Hi [First Name],

Following up to see if this interests you?

"Copy and paste details from the initial email" OR at the very least, send it in the original email thread. Remember, great candidates constantly receive offers.

Tip: Effective Follow up Techniques Consider using touchpoints from an earlier email, or reiterating company or position highlights to grab their attention and prompt a response.

Sample #2

Hi [First Name],

You interviewed with our team about a year ago and can the time you withdrew from our process.

I wanted to see if you would be open to interviewing again?

I truly feel your background and the company culture would be a great fit, hence my persistence.

If you could take a moment to respond with the following, I would greatly appreciate it.

- ☐ You're interested but prefer a follow up in 1-2 months.
- ☐ You're not at all interested and ask that I leave you alone.

This will let me know how to proceed. Thanks so much!

Consider connecting across multiple channels

For instance, if you found a candidate on LinkedIn or Facebook, take some time to check out their recent posts and respond with a like or comment. This approach has the potential to accomplish a few things:

- It shows you're interested in learning more about them.

- It can also gently remind them of you,

- You might discover a mutual connection that will provide a great reason for a follow up (or even an initial outreach). Conversely, it equips you with additional information to further personalize your messages.

Sample #3

Hi [First Name],

Your post on [Topic] came to my attention through a mutual connection on LinkedIn. You've shared some insightful ideas that I have found very interesting. Thank you. You seem very enthusiastic about [Matter].

It only emphasized my thoughts on how you would be a great match for the [Role] I mentioned in my previous email.

Is tomorrow a good time to discuss this opportunity with you?

Sample #4

I sent you an email last week but I didn't hear back. I wanted to see if you still had any interest in pursuing our team's role. This might not be the best timing – but just let me know either way.

Sample #6

As mentioned, I'd love to set up a 20-30-minute call for us to talk through your background, interests, and share more about (company) and our (specific) team in particular!

Could you please send me your resume along with a few dates/times that work to connect this week or next?

Hiring Manager Templates

Have your hiring manager follow up with the candidate directly via email or InMail. Have them use the same follow up message while also mentioning they are the hiring manager and interested in meeting the candidate, etc.

Sample #1

Hello, I'm [name] – a product and software development leader at [company] in the Delivery Technology team.

I'm writing as I'm building out a new organization and need to hire smart, fun people to come along. I certainly understand if you're not looking to make a move from [company], but I'd still love to just connect with you and hear more about your last few years as well as share a bit of what we're up to.

For more context, in the last ~4 years [company] has built out our own logistics delivery network (think: Uber for Shipping Tech).

The new teams I'm building are focused on a new, high-profile initiative to scale this network quickly in 2023. Please let me know if you are open to having a chat. Hope to hear from you.

Sample #2

I hope your week is going great. I was impressed with your recent MBA work at (school) along with your recent development experience at (company).

I'm reaching out because I support our Technology team in both Boston and Seattle and we are looking for talented and experienced engineers like yourself to join our growing team! We are working on several exciting initiatives and you'd be able to help in developing large scale distributed technology solutions and innovate new ideas to our business.

I'm sure you are super happy at this time, but I would think it might be worth reaching out to see if you're open to hearing about opportunities within my team?

I'd love to chat to learn about you, share more insights about my team, and see if there could be possible alignment now or in the future!

Sample #3

I came across one of your previous applications for one of my teams Software Engineer opportunities and I was really impressed with your background and recent work at (company).

My team supports different Engineering teams within (company).

I'd love to set up an initial 20-minute call to learn more about you and tell you more about the opportunities within our division.

Sample #4

Hi (name),
We are working on several exciting green light development initiatives and we own several customer facing applications and products that you would create cutting edge UIs for.

You'd be joining an innovative, cross platform, and customer-obsessed team building fascinating new web services and products!

Let me know if you would be open to having a call soon!

Sample #5

Hi (name),

My name is (name) and I'm a manager that supports our Technology services with (company) and I'm looking for experienced and talented engineers like yourself to join our growing teams!

Our division develops the technology that is responsible for the optimization and automation.

We are working on several exciting initiatives tied to supporting the rapid evolution of our network and you'd be able to help in developing large scale distributed technology solutions and innovate new ideas to our business.

Would you be open to having a call?

Tip: Thank them if they respond and decline your message. They might know someone actively looking for a new role. Take the time to "thank them" and ask for a referral.

Let me know should anything change on your end. Would you happen to know anyone in your network with a similar background as you looking for work?

Chapter 6: Email Sequencing Campaigns

Now that you have created your templates, it's time to automate them via email sequencing tools. It's yet another powerful time saver and with the right email automation tool, it allows you to stay in contact with candidates without manually hitting send every step of the way.

The concept of a drip campaign is quite simple. In this instance, we're talking about email marketing, where a drip campaign delivers a sequence of messages at certain, pre-specified points in time to help boost engagement and clicks. Recruiters can use these tools to send out scheduled emails and follows to attract and engage a lead.

Drip campaigns are considered more effective than the traditional (Mail Merge) email blasts that recruiters have been sending for years now. That's because drip campaigns enable you to get super personal, targeting specific prospects right in their inbox at just at the right time.

When it comes to drip campaigns, response and click rates are the number one way to measure success, and truly the only metrics that matter the most. An engagement from the recipient truly means that you're sequence campaign has successfully worked.

Constructing an Effective Email Sequence:

Constructing an effective sequence happens by trial and error. You will need to slowly experiment on a sequence to see what works and make improvements along the way. Your email should consist of the following components:

Subject Line(s):

This is the line your recipient will see before they even open your email. It drives their split-second decisions to read or ignore it.

Connection:

The first line in the email is what should grab them to finish reading so they don't bounce back to their inbox. It should immediately connect to the subject line that got them to open the email. If you sound like a robot then odds are your email will get sent to a spam junk folder.

Question:

Once you have established a connection, ask a question. Be clear and upfront. If you have an open position, just say it. Be precise about what you have and create urgency by asking for a response in the next 2-3 days. Make them seem valued and that you need a response from them as soon as possible.

Email Engagement:
Once the lead responses do you have additional follow up email templates to address questions or concerns? Also, whichever tool you choose will be a factor in this. Most email sequences will stop or pause of the lead responses to the direct email.

When writing your email, remember to focus on common ground to build trust. Including a sincere compliment is also very effective.

Ultimately, you need to focus on personalization, which you can still do even if you're marketing at scale.

For instance, if you're reaching out to more than 10 people, you can save time while still maximizing effectiveness by focusing on deeply personalizing the first email each person will receive. From there, you can let automation do more of the work for you, saving time while still making sure that the most important message–that first email that needs to elicit that first response–is as personal as possible.

Also, remember that simply including an organization or brand name doesn't mean an email has been personalized. You need to do some digging and go beyond that if you truly want the person reading your email to feel that all-important connection that tells them you have spent time considering them as an individual.

Here is an example of email sequence campaign:

Here's a possible recruiter email sequence of four emails to attract a candidate for a job opening:

Email 1 - Introduction and Job Description
Subject: [Company Name] - [Job Title] opening

Hi [Candidate's Name],

My name is [Your Name], and I'm a recruiter at [Company Name]. I found your profile on [source] and noticed that you have [relevant skills/experience]. We have an exciting job opportunity for a [Job Title] that we think you would be perfect for. The role is located in [City], and it comes with a competitive salary and benefits package. Here's a link to the job description: [Job Description Link].

If you're interested in learning more about the position, please let me know, and we can schedule a call at your convenience.

Best,
[Your Name]

Email 2 - Company Culture and Values
Subject: [Company Name] - Our Culture and Values

Hi [Candidate's Name],

I hope you're doing well. I wanted to follow up on my previous email and tell you a bit more about [Company Name]. Our company is dedicated to [Mission Statement], and we pride ourselves on [Company Value 1], [Company Value 2], and [Company Value 3].

We believe that [Value 1] and [Value 2] are critical to our success and create an environment where everyone can thrive. We are looking for people who share our values and are committed to making a positive impact. If you're interested in learning more about our company culture, please let me know, and we can schedule a call.

Best,
[Your Name]

Email 3 - Employee Testimonials and Benefits
Subject: [Company Name] - Employee Testimonials and Benefits

Hi [Candidate's Name],

I wanted to share some testimonials from our current employees to give you a sense of what it's like to work at [Company Name]. Here are some of the things they've said:

"We're a close-knit team, and we support each other in everything we do."
"The company benefits are incredible. I've never had a benefits package like this before."

"The company encourages professional development, and I've learned so much since I started working here."

In addition to our great company culture, we offer a competitive salary and benefits package that includes [Benefits 1], [Benefits 2], and [Benefits 3]. If you're interested in learning more about the benefits we offer, please let me know, and we can schedule a call.

Best,
[Your Name]

Email 4 - Final Call to Action
Subject: [Company Name] - Last Chance to Apply

Hi [Candidate's Name],

I wanted to follow up one last time to see if you were interested in the [Job Title] opening at [Company Name]. We are still looking for the right candidate, and we believe you could be a great fit.

If you have any questions or concerns, please let me know, and we can schedule a call to discuss further. If you're ready to take

the next step, you can apply directly
through our website: [Application Link].

Thank you for your time and consideration,
and I look forward to hearing from you
soon.

Best,
[Your Name]

Chapter 7: How to Use Mail Merge

As a Recruiter, outreach and follow-up are at the core of your position, but they both involve a lot of tedious, manual, monotonous labor to do it right.

Fortunately, lots of "secret" tools are out there that could help take away some of that touch work. Mail merge from Microsoft Word or Excel is one excellent example.

What is mail merge?

Looking to customize a document, such as an email or newsletter? A mail merge is the answer. With a mail merge, you can instantly and automatically personalize any number of documents for all your recipients, sparing you lots of manual labor.

For instance, if you're sending cold emails, you can use a mail merge to add a unique greeting, mention each candidate's name, and even include their job position, company, and other relevant details. That means you just need to type up a template first, and a mail merge will instantly insert all their info from a spreadsheet. In other words, it's a massive time saver.

How to Use Mail Merges

The first step to using mail merge is getting the two components setup. The first is the template file, which is the document you send out (such as your email) with the placeholders where you want to insert the personalized data and the second is the data file, which is a Microsoft Excel spreadsheet or Google Sheets file where you organize the personalization data.

When you open your template file in Word or Excel and navigate to the Mail Merge feature, it will prompt you to select the location of your data file, and it will do the rest of the work for you, filling in the placeholders of your template with the data for each recipient and generating a personalized email or letter for everyone in your list.

Mail Merge is the process of compiling a list of a large number of contacts that you want to email all at once instead of one at a time. You can somewhat personalize your messaging with a mail merge which is highly recommended as you do not want to come off as spamming candidates.

CanSpam

Mass emails for cold outreach do not have an automatic unsubscribe option at the bottom. I recommend adding a message to your emails to avoid any legal problems.

At [Company Name], we pride ourselves on crafting personalized emails and avoid using mass email tools. However, we understand that our emails may not be of interest to everyone, and we respect your decision to opt out of further communication.

If you no longer wish to receive emails from us, simply reply to this email and let us know. We will promptly remove you from our mailing list and ensure that you don't receive any further emails from us.

CAN-SPAM Act is a federal law in the United States that sets rules for commercial email messages. It's not something that recruiters can "avoid" as it's a legal requirement they must comply with.

To ensure compliance with the CAN-SPAM Act, recruiters can take the following steps:

1. Include a clear and accurate subject line that reflects the content of the email message.

2. Use a valid "From" address that identifies the company or individual sending the message.

3. Include a physical address for the sender in the email message.

4. Provide a clear and conspicuous way for recipients to opt-out of future email messages.

5. Honor opt-out requests promptly and accurately.

6. Monitor the actions of third-party email marketers who may be sending emails on their behalf.

By following these guidelines, recruiters can ensure compliance with the CAN-SPAM Act and avoid potential legal penalties for non-compliance.

Here's how to step up a Mail Merge using Excel / Word: / Outlook

Preliminary Work:

Compile a list of all the candidate's information you want to reach out to in excel. You must include first name and email at a minimum, but you may add other personalized filters such as current company, skill set, location, etc.

For example:

	A	B	C
	First Name	**Email**	**Company**
1			
2	Vegas	vegas.miller@gmail.com	Leidos
3	Nathan	natem559@gmail.com	Hollstadt
4	Vaishali	vaishalikumar@hotmail.com	Lifetouch
5	Callie	callie.f.bensel@gmail.com	Upsie
6	Thomas	thomasohagen@gmail.com	Optum
7	Joseph	jwitthuhn@uwalumni.com	Thomson Reuters
8	John	jhnkotz@gmail.com	SmartThings
9	Jacob	jacobrdalton@gmail.com	Sentera
10	Charles	chajohnson10@gmail.com	Express Scripts
11	Michael	mpcitak@gmail.com	IDeaS Revenue
12	Nicholas	boldt.nicholas@gmail.com	NextEra Analytics
13	Chad	cmrobinson@gmail.com	Virtuwell
14	Joseph	jayr86@gmail.com	Target

Step 1: Once you have all the candidates you wish to email in your excel spreadsheet, save the document and open Microsoft Word. Insert the template you wish to use for the body of your email and add in the column names where your personalized information will go (name, company, etc.)

Once complete, on the top click "Mailings" and then "Start Mail Merge" and then from the drop down hit "Step-by-Step Mail Merge Wizard." Once you hit "Step-by-Step Mail Merge Wizard", a column titled "Mail Merge" will appear on the right-hand side. Click "Email messages" and then click (step 1 of 6) "Next: Starting document" at the bottom of the screen.

Step 2: Click (step 2 of 6) "Next: Select recipients" at the bottom right.

Next, click "Use an existing list" and then hit "Browse" to find and double click the Excel document with the contact information you compiled initially.
Once you double click your document, a window titled "Select Table" will pop up. Click "OK."

Next, another widow will pop up titled "Mail Merge Recipients". Assure the column headers are correct (Name, Company, Email, etc.) and then click "OK."

Step 3: On the bottom right of the screen (Step
3 of 6), click "Next: Write your email message".

Under "Write your email message", click "Greeting line..." A window titled "Insert Greeting Line" will then pop up where you can choose your preferences. Because in the example template "Hey" is already included as the greeting and a comma is also already included after "Name", I will choose "(none)" for both options in addition to "Greeting line for invalid recipient names". For the person's name, I chose the full name "Joshua."

After you have these selections made BEFORE you hit OK, click on "Match Fields."

Once you hit Match Fields, a window will pop up titled "Match Fields." This is a very important step to ensure the fields in the excel spreadsheet convert over accurately to the Word doc template (in this example we would be looking to make sure name, company, and email match).

Check all personalized fields to assure the columns on the left-hand side and match the ones on the right which represent your excel sheet. Scroll down to assure the email matches as well. Hit "OK."

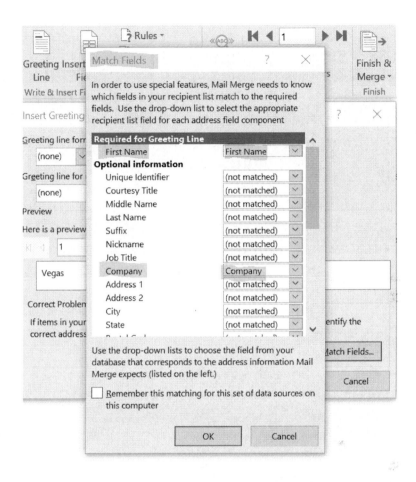

Once you hit "OK", a "Greeting Line" field will appear wherever you have your cursor, so be sure to place it next to "Name" at the top of your template. This is the field that will populate each candidate name from the excel spreadsheet. Go ahead and delete the "name" text as this field will populate by itself.

Next, we need to insert a field to populate the "company" column in our spreadsheet. Make sure your cursor is by "company" on your Word template. Click "More Items" on the right-hand column. A window will pop up titled "Insert Merge Field", and you will want to select "company" and then hit "insert."

Once you have done this, close out of the window, and you will see that a "company" field has populated where you had your cursor.

Delete the company text next to the field as this field will populate each candidate's company per the column in the spreadsheet. Now that we have our email populated with the correct fields, we will move on to Step 4.

Step 4: On the bottom right of the screen (Step 4 of 6), click "Next: Preview your email message".

Once you hit preview, you will see that your email template will be populated with the first candidate's name and company information. In the top right column, you can click through each one of your recipients to preview how each email will look and assure the information has populated correctly before moving on to the next step.

Step 5: On the bottom right of the screen (Step 5 of 6), click "Next: Complete the merge".

You will then click "Electronic Mail" under the Mail Merge tab on the right side. A window will pop up with message options which should look as follows:

To: Email

Subject Line: Input your own email subject line that will appear on all emails sent to candidates

Mail format: HTML Send records: ALL BEWARE – Once you hit "OK", the emails will begin to send, so make sure everything is how you want before you hit the OK button!

Step 6: All Done! Go to our Outlook account to see the emails all sent. 😊

Using Outlook contacts as a data source for a Mail Merge:

To utilize Outlook's mail merge feature and remain connected, follow the steps below:

1. Open Outlook and go to Contacts.

2. Choose the names you want to include, or skip this step to use the entire address book.

3. Click Home > Mail Merge

4. Select the options you prefer and click OK. If you plan to reuse the same set of contacts, choose Permanent file and give the list a name.

5. In Word, on the Mailings tab, insert merge fields that pull information from the Outlook contacts list into your document. The Address Block merge field is suitable for envelopes and labels, while Greeting Line is great for personalizing letters and emails.

6. Add any desired text to the documents, envelopes, labels, or emails, such as the body of a form letter.

7. Preview the results and navigate through each personalized document, envelope, label, or email using the Next or Previous record button for mail merge preview results.

8. To finish the merge, choose Finish & Merge in the Finish group, and then click Print Documents or Send E-mail Messages.

9. Save the merge document to reuse it without resetting anything up. The merge document will remain connected to the data source.

10. When you want to run it again, for instance, for another batch of envelopes to the same people, open the document in Word by selecting File > Open and then choosing Yes when prompted by Word to maintain the connection.

Doing a Mail Merge in Google Documents:

The Mail Merge for Google Docs™ & Google Sheets™ add-on is a free and straightforward way to generate documents, letters, emails, and print envelopes. It lets you export to PDF, Word, or print right within Google Docs™ without any advertising or watermarks.

This add-on is ideal for mail merging documents within Google Workspace™ and allows you to create hundreds of personalized emails, letters, and envelopes from a mailing list, as well as merge documents like reports, certificates, and more. The Mail Merge Wizard guides you through the process of creating merged documents in Google Docs™ from a Google Spreadsheet mailing list.

How to use the add-on tool:
Mail Merge is a technique used to create personalized batches of documents for each recipient, such as a form letter that addresses each recipient by name. A data source, such as a Google Sheets™ spreadsheet, is associated with the document, and placeholders, known as merge fields, are used to tell Google Docs™ where to include information from the data source. This makes it possible to merge emails, letters, envelopes, or labels.

To create a mail merge document in Google Docs™, follow the steps below:

1. Open Google Docs™ (https://docs.new)
2. Create a template document, such as an empty invoice template or a student grade report.
3. Click on the Mail Merge button in the right sidebar.
4. Choose the document type, such as letters, envelopes, labels, or emails.
5. Select recipients and choose which spreadsheet to pull data from in the sidebar.
6. Insert merge fields to personalize each document.
7. Generate the documents.

8. Download them as Docs, PDF, or Word.

To create a mail merge from a Google Sheets™, follow these steps:

1. Open Google Sheets™ (https://sheets.new)
2. Click on the Mail Merge button in the right sidebar.
3. Choose the document to merge and create a template document in Google Docs™ beforehand, such as an empty invoice template or a student grade report.
4. Choose the document type, such as letters, envelopes, labels, or emails. The recipients will be the people listed in the current tab of Google Sheets™.
5. Generate the documents.
6. Download them as Docs, PDF, or Word.
7. Mail Merge for Google Docs™ is a free alternative to other mail merge tools, such as Yet Another Mail Merge (YAMM), Gmass, Mail Merge with Attachments, and Mailmeteor. It comes with examples of mail merge letters and various templates, such as a birthday invitation, form letter,

resume, annual report, certificate, and Google Docs™ templates for students.

Mail merge with Gmail & Google Sheets using a script:

To use this solution, you first create a Gmail draft template with placeholders that match the data in a Sheets spreadsheet. The column headers in the sheet serve as placeholder tags. A script then sends the information for each placeholder from the spreadsheet to the corresponding location of the placeholder tag in your email draft.

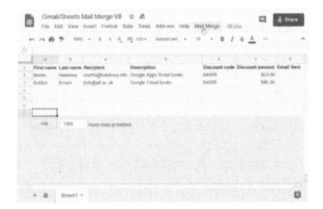

This solution utilizes the following Apps Script services:

- Gmail service: retrieves, reads, and sends the draft email to your recipients.

- Spreadsheet service: fills in the email placeholders with the personalized information for each recipient.

Before using this sample, make sure you have the following prerequisites:

- A Google Account (Google Workspace accounts may require administrator approval).
- A web browser with internet access.

To set up the script, follow these steps:

1. Create the Apps Script project by making a copy of the Gmail/Sheets Mail Merge sample spreadsheet: https://docs.google.com/spreadsheets/d/1 2b1oEDXSrwwlU4c3C7khFYQSt-pp0ujE3HqbehBm5z0/edit?usp=sharing

2. In the copied spreadsheet, update the "Recipients" column with the email addresses to be used in the mail merge. You can also customize the data by adding, editing, or removing columns.

3. Create an email draft in your Gmail account and use placeholders that correspond to column names in the spreadsheet. The placeholders are enclosed in curly braces (e.g. {{First name}}). Note that placeholders are case-

sensitive and must exactly match the column headers. If you format the text in the email, you must also format the placeholder brackets.

4. To run the script, click "Mail Merge" > "Send Emails" in the spreadsheet. If necessary, refresh the page to display the custom menu. When prompted, authorize the script and paste the email template subject line.

5. If you need to review the Apps Script code for this solution review this link: https://github.com/googleworkspace/apps-script-samples/blob/main/solutions/automations/mail-merge/Code.js

Using Chatpgt in your Mail Merge Outreach:

Cargo Tool

Are you struggling to personalize your emails at scale? What if you could create thousands of unique and personalized emails in just a few minutes? With the help of Cargo, a Google Sheets extension, and ChatGPT, an open-source language model developed by OpenAI, you can easily create unique emails without the hassle of crafting each one individually.

Cargo is a software add-on for Google Sheets that streamlines outbound organizations by retrieving company information, generating personalized email introductions, and cleaning data lists. To use Cargo with ChatGPT, you need to add the extension to Google Sheets and obtain an API key from OpenAI.

ChatGPT is an artificial intelligence model trained on a massive amount of text data that generates human-like text responses. It can be integrated into various applications to enable advanced language-based functionality and improve the overall user experience.

To integrate Cargo with ChatGPT, follow these simple steps:

1. Install the Cargo extension from https://www.getcargo.io/ai-for-sheets
2. Sign up for OpenAI and obtain your API key at https://beta.openai.com/account/api-keys

3. Copy and paste your API key in the Cargo extension tab in Google Sheets.

4. Start personalizing your outreach based on the input given to ChatGPT. The more input ChatGPT has, the more effective the personalization will be.

If you scrape your lead lists directly from LinkedIn using Sales Navigator and Phantombuster, you can use the LinkedIn bio column as input to get personalized icebreakers. To do this, follow these steps:

1. Open your Cargo Extension in Google Sheets and select the pre-made template named "Icebreaker Generator."

2. Input the name of your LinkedIn bio column as a custom parameter using "{{" brackets. Be careful with spelling mistakes as the tool is case-sensitive.

3. Click on "Preview" to get a sample result before running the AI automation on your list. If the result looks good, click on the "V" in the upper-right of the add-on.

4. Select the rows you want to run the automation on and choose the column to display the results on. Click "RUN."

As with any new tool or feature, it may take some playing around with mail merge to get it perfect and to understand all you can do with it. The best place to start is by typing up a template, or perhaps just grabbing a version of an email you recently sent, and then playing around with your data file to see all the placeholders you can come up with.

As a recruiter, you can easily populate a data file automatically by using the information you already scraped from LinkedIn and other websites about your candidates. For instance, beyond their name, you might put in details about the company they work for, their current title, where they went to school, and so on.

Once you have your two files created, go ahead and see how mail merge works. To save you time, it even gives you a "Preview" option before your prompt it to generate all the personalized versions, so make use of that to avoid errors.

Final Thoughts

A recruiter email mail merge is a great way to send personalized email messages to a large number of potential candidates. Here are some tips to help you create a successful recruiter email mail merge:

Segment your audience: Start by segmenting your email list based on factors such as job title, location, industry, and experience level. This will help you create targeted messages that are more likely to resonate with your audience.

Personalize your messages: Use the candidate's name and other relevant details, such as their experience and skills, to make the message more personal and relevant. This can help to increase the chances of the candidate engaging with your message.

Use a clear subject line: Your subject line should be clear, concise, and relevant to the message. Avoid using generic subject lines that could be mistaken for spam.

Keep your message brief: Your message should be short and to the point. Avoid using overly complex language or industry jargon that could be confusing to the candidate.

Include a clear call-to-action: Your message should include a clear call-to-action that encourages the candidate to take the next step. This could be to apply for the job, schedule a call, or learn more about the company.

Test your messages: Before sending your messages, test them to make sure they render correctly and are free of errors. This can help to ensure that your messages are well-received and that you don't miss out on potential candidates.

Follow up: If you don't hear back from a candidate after the first email, follow up with a second or third message. This can help to increase the chances of the candidate engaging with your message and taking the next step. However, be sure not to overdo it and risk annoying the candidate.

ChatGPT AI Writing Tool

For years now there has been a prediction about how AI is going to take over recruiting. So far there have been some tools that have helped recruiters be more efficient and better, but most of the tools out there so far have not lived up to the hype.

In comes, Open AI's Chat GPT-3 which I know is not going to replace any recruiters at the moment, but it's the best AI tool that has been released to the public.

How can you use this tool with messaging?

Use AI to reach out to potential candidates through personalized emails or messages, inviting them to apply for a job or to learn more about the organization.

Once you create an account you can ask this AI tool virtually any type of question. So, I decided to ask it how to write effective recruiter messages and here's the result.

[Write a Short Example of Outreach to a Potential Candidate About a Data Science Job...]

Hi [Candidate],

I hope this message finds you well. My name is [Your Name] and I am a recruiter with [Company Name]. I came across your LinkedIn profile and was impressed by your background in data science.

I wanted to reach out to see if you might be interested in a data science opportunity that we have available at our company. The role involves working on a range of data-driven projects, using a variety of tools and techniques to analyze and interpret data.

We are looking for someone with strong problem-solving skills and a passion for data.

I would love to speak with you more about this opportunity and see if it might be a good fit for you.

If you are interested, please don't hesitate to reach out to me to schedule a call at your convenience.

Best regards,
[Your Name]

The ChatGPT AI is truly amazing!

Summary

Overall, the key to finding top-talent and holding their attention from the moment you schedule the interview until you share the "You're Hired" announcement, and everything in between has been covered in this eBook.

When you use the templates, we've provided and implement the protocols of understanding the positions and candidates, you'll have all the necessary tools to become a top producer. And, as advancements in technology and AI tools continue to become available, we'll keep you updated!

Here's a summary of what you should have learned from reading this book:

Make It About Them
So often, recruiter emails focus on how the recipient can help them or their company, rather than how the candidate can benefit from the deal. By simply changing the pronouns from "us" to "you," it gives attention to the candidate.

Your initial email should be presented in a friendly tone and in first person to make it more personalized. When you can, make "small talk" that's relevant, complementary, and shows you've done your research.

Steer Clear of Scripted Email
While templates certainly have a place in streamlining your processes, avoid using generic templates. Besides them being a turnoff to the talented candidate that likely receives multiple recruiting emails every day, they can also force your emails into spam.

Take the time to create your own unique templates that can easily be personalized. Leave blank space so that you can come up with truly individual emails for each candidate you're reaching out to.

Use Attention Grabbing Subject Lines
The subject line of an email means the difference between your email being opened, ignored, or sent to spam. Best practices include creating a subject line that is short and to the point. It should contain less than 10 words or be between 25-30 characters.

You should also steer clear of certain terms that are known to trigger spam such as "exclusive offer," "opportunity," and "guaranteed." These terms will also turnoff candidates for sounding too vague or salesy. Try to keep the tone personal and direct.

Send Mobile-Friendly Emails
Being mobile-friendly does not refer to the technical aspects of your email. Rather, it's about the words you use. Whenever you are drafting an email to prospects, send it to yourself first to see how it looks on a mobile device. The subject line should be short, clean, and easily viewable on a mobile phone.

The email itself shouldn't be too long, either, as no one wants to read a book — especially when checking from their phone, which is where most candidates open their emails.

Include a Call-To-Action
An introduction email should be simple and enticing. Remember, the candidate doesn't know you, so a lengthy email is not ideal.

However, before ending your email with a warm sign-off, be sure to include a call-to-action designed to prompt them to respond in a timely manner.

Always Follow Up

Don't let the lack of response to your first email discourage you from following up. In fact, successful recruiters follow up a minimum of 3-6 times.

Because your primary goal is to establish communication with a candidate, a few friendly nudges via follow up emails can increase your chances of success!

Finally, the goal of your recruiting emails is to capture the attention of the recipient and eventually build a rapport. This all boils down to becoming skilled in your email creations.

Conclusion:

I hope you've gained insights crafting messages and have found value from these chapters.

I've written on several topics within recruiting and have received so many kind notes and messages from recruiters across the world. I can't thank you enough for that. It has enlightened and humbled me greatly.

I would appreciate it if you would take the time to write an honest review about the book on Amazon so that others can also benefit from this publication.

Note: Many of the recruiter templates recommended have been shared with me by other recruiters in the field. It's hard to give credit to messages that have been widely shared. I truly appreciate recruiters willing to share some great examples with me to make this project possible.

Please follow WizardSourcer.com for my latest updates.

Appendix:

Builtin.com
GetResponse.com
Hubspot.com
Indeed.com
Lifewire.com
LinkedIn.com
Mailmunch.com
Recruitflow.com
Statisitics.com
Chat.openai.com

Made in the USA
Las Vegas, NV
08 December 2024

81ba649f-38db-4cd0-99af-265e01cc8d27R01